FOOD FROM MANY LANDS

Beverley Birch

Macdonald Educational

How to use this book

First, look at the contents page opposite. Read the chapter list to see if it includes the subject you want. The list tells you what each page is about. You can then find the page with the information you need.

If you want to know about one particular thing, look it up in the index on page 31. For example, if you want to know about markets, the index tells you that there is something about them on pages 18 and 19. The index also lists the pictures in the book.

When you read this book, you will find some unusual words. The glossary on page 30 explains what they mean.

Series Editor
Margaret Conroy

Book Editor
Barbara Tombs

Production
Susan Mead

Picture Research
Caroline Mitchell

Factual Adviser
Sarah Hobson

Reading Consultant
Amy Gibbs
Inner London Education Authority
Centre for Language in Primary
Education

Series Design
Robert Mathias/Anne Isseyegh

Book Design
Anne Isseyegh

Teacher Panel
Peter Denman
Lynne McCoombe
Ann Merriman

Illustrations
Ann Baum/Linda Rogers Associates
Pages 6-7, 11, 12-13, 22-23, 24-25
Nichola Boraman Pages 8-9, 28
David Eaton Front cover
Shirley Willis Pages 14-15, 16-17, 20-21

Photographs
Cover: family meal in China

Nick Birch: 17; 18
Daily Telegraph Colour Library: 27
Richard and Sally Greenhill: cover; 9; 10
ICI Agricultural Division: 29
Bury Peerless: 11
FAO/UN: 8 left and right
Waitrose (a branch of the John Lewis
Partnership): 19
ZEFA: 7; 12; 26

CONTENTS

EATING   6-13
Food and you   6-7
Eating for health   8-9
Food for enjoyment   10-11
What do you eat?   12-13

FINDING FOOD   14-19
What is food?   14-15
Farming and fishing   16-17
Buying and selling   18-19

PREPARING FOOD   20-25
How we cook   20-21
Preserving and processing food   22-23
Meals around the world   24-25

WHERE ARE WE GOING?   26-29
Hunger in the world   26-27
What can be done?   28-29

GLOSSARY, BOOKS TO READ   30

INDEX   31

EATING

Food and you

How much time do you spend eating each day? You probably eat in the morning, again at midday and in the evening. You may have snacks between these meals. Have you ever wondered why you spend all this time eating?

You may also have noticed pictures of foods which you've never seen in real life. Have you ever wondered why you can't buy them in your local shops? Or why some foods you eat come from very distant countries, but others are grown locally? And why do some cost a lot, while others are cheap?

This book will help to explain these things. It is about why food is so important to us, and what happens if we don't get enough of the right kind of food.

It will show you why so many different foods are found in different parts of the world, and why people prepare their meals in such a variety of ways. It will also help you to understand why your family eats only some foods, and why you have never had the chance to taste others.

Food is one of the main things we share, by eating in the company of family or friends.

People also share the work of obtaining food. More food can be produced like this.

Eating for health

When you feel hungry, your body is telling you that it wants food. Food gives it energy to move and think, and building materials to repair itself and grow. Your body takes many substances called nutrients from the food you eat, and if it does not get enough of these different nutrients, then it cannot work properly or stay healthy.

Different nutrients are found in different types of foods. You need to eat something from each type to make sure that you get enough of each nutrient. There are millions of people in the world who do not get enough nutrients. If they have too little food they starve and if their diet is not made up of enough different types of food, they become ill.

Cereals, bread, beans, peas, lentils, nuts, give you energy from nutrients called carbohydrates and give your body building materials from the nutrient called protein.

These food groups contain all the nutrients you need. You should eat something from each group every day.

On the left a baby who is not getting enough nutrients, and the same baby after 10 months of eating the right kinds of foods.

8

Fruit and vegetables
(eaten cooked and raw)
give many nutrients,
including vitamins, to
keep you healthy and
fight disease.

Meat, poultry, fish,
eggs, help you grow and
give your body the building
material called protein.
Vegetarians need to eat
milk foods or cereals instead.

Butter, margarine, fats and
oils give you energy from
their carbohydrates and
fats and contain vitamins.

Milk, cheese, yoghurt
and other milk foods
have many nutrients
including calcium to give
you strong bones and
teeth.

Eating more than your
body needs will make it
unhealthy and stop it
working properly.

Food for enjoyment

Did you know that the word companion means someone with whom you share bread? It comes from the Latin words *cum* (with) and *panis* (bread). Offering food to someone has always been a way of showing friendship, just as nowadays you might invite a friend to tea or to a party meal.

Food gives us a feeling of comfort and warmth. It is not just something we need to eat — we also enjoy it. We celebrate important occasions like birthdays and weddings with a special meal or we may go out for a meal for a treat. We give someone food as a gift; for example a box of chocolates, or a food which is too expensive to buy normally, like an unusual jam, a rich cake, or exotic fruit.

Families often get together at festivals to enjoy a special meal. All festive occasions have their own particular foods. Here a family eats a traditional English Christmas dinner.

At the Hindu festival of Divali, specially made sweetmeats and cakes are offered to the Goddess Lakshmi because people believe that she likes them.

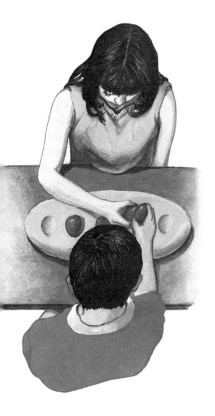

Here Greek children are cracking eggs which decorate their Easter bread. Festive foods may have a meaning and eggs often stand for new life in spring.

Festivals are always times for feasting, whether on religious holidays like Christmas, or festivals marking the year's changing seasons such as the end of winter, or the harvesting of crops. An enormous feast often follows a fast, which is a time when religion forbids eating certain things, or eating at certain times as in the Muslim fast of Ramadan.

What do you eat?

If you live in Europe you are unlikely to eat pawpaw because you won't be able to grow it, or find it easily in shops. Even if you can, it will cost a lot, so you are more likely to eat apples or pears, which can be grown easily or bought cheaply.

People only eat the foods they can obtain. The land and the climate will affect which foods a country can produce. Rice, for example, needs water and warmth, so people living in colder, drier countries where rice cannot grow, must buy it from those places where it can.

Many religions forbid people to eat some things. Hindus believe that the cow is sacred, and will not kill it, but in some countries cattle arc an important source of meat.

You may not eat all the foods available to you. Your family may not have the money to buy some foods. You may not like certain things or you may think they're bad for you. Your religion may forbid you to eat some food. If you are a Muslim or a Jew you will not eat pork. Some people think eating any meat is wrong.

Insects, grubs, hedgehogs, slugs, frogs, chicken feet, snails are all food to people somewhere in the world. What foods do you eat? Are there any you won't eat?

People will be able to eat plenty of fish if they live near seas and rivers. This fish market is in Portugal, where both dried and fresh fish are common food. You can see the dried fish hanging up.

FINDING FOOD

What is food?

Food comes from plants or animals. Whatever it looks like on your plate, it will have come from one of these sources. We eat the leaves of plants (like cabbage); their roots and tubers (carrots, potatoes, yams, cassavas); seeds (cereals, beans); fruit (peaches, tomatoes, cucumbers); stems (celery, sugar cane). We also eat the meat, milk and eggs of some animals.

Food can be bought fresh, or preserved and processed in some way, as shown below. Which of these have you eaten? Which come from plants and which from animals or fish?

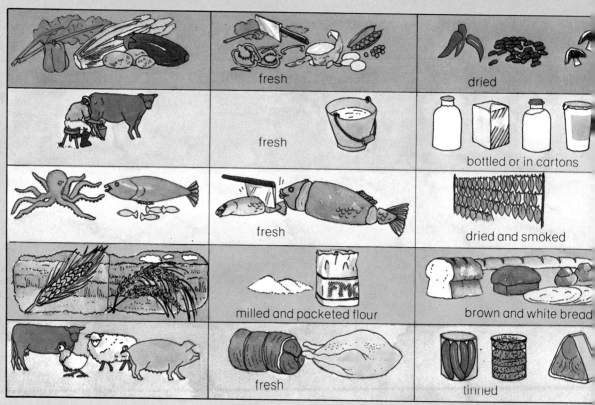

fresh
dried

fresh
bottled or in cartons

fresh
dried and smoked

milled and packeted flour
brown and white bread

fresh
tinned

Every country has one main food which people eat with most of their meals and this is called their staple food.
Usually it is a plant which is easily produced in their own country.

The staple foods in many countries come from cereal plants. For example, bread made from wheat is the staple in many cooler parts of the world, like Britain. Rice is the staple in south-east Asia.

In other countries easily-grown vegetables are the staple food, like the potato in many parts of Europe and South America.

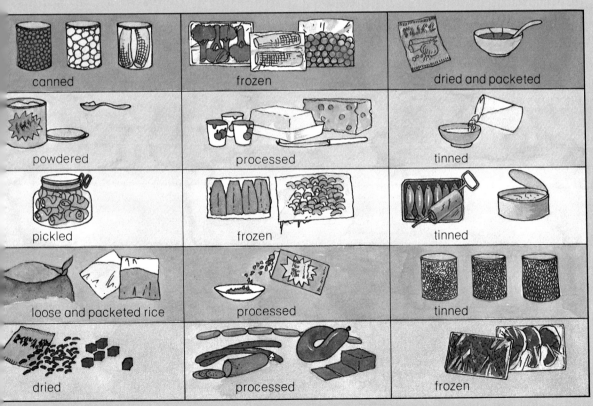

canned	frozen	dried and packeted
powdered	processed	tinned
pickled	frozen	tinned
loose and packeted rice	processed	tinned
dried	processed	frozen

Farming and fishing

Most food comes from animals and plants which have been produced specially for eating, or from fish caught in seas, rivers and lakes.

People farm in many different ways all over the world. Some people milk cows by hand, use ox-drawn ploughs or keep hens which roam freely. Others have ploughs drawn by tractor, and machines to plant and harvest crops or milk cows.

Not all crops can be harvested by machine. We pick most fruit by hand from plants which have to remain growing for the next season. But cereals can be harvested by machine because the whole plant is cut down.

Both these Japanese farmers are harvesting rice: the one on the right is using a sickle; the other is using a harvesting machine. Whether farmers use machines often depends on whether they have enough money to buy them.

In Europe, people fish from boats like this, using nets worked by machine.

Fishermen use boats and fishing nets of many shapes and sizes, from tiny canoes and handnets to huge factory ships where the fish are cleaned and frozen on the ship.

This trawler drags its net behind it, scooping up fish. Then a crane hauls in the net and drops the fish on deck, where they are cleaned and packed in ice.

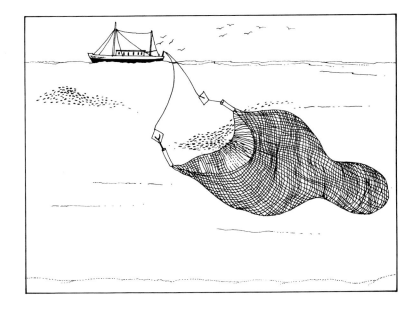

Buying and selling

Many people produce food mainly for themselves. They sell any food which is left over at local markets, so they can buy other things they need. But most of the world's food is produced specially for sale. Some is sold nearby, whilst some is sent all over the country to be sold.

Some food is even produced just for sale to other countries, possibly very distant ones.

Many markets are held in the open air, like this one. Customers buy what they want from the different stalls. A lot of the food sold is fresh.

A supermarket is a kind of general food shop. Customers help themselves and pay for everything as they leave. Supermarkets sell many canned, frozen and packaged foods.

Most people buy much of their food, and so everywhere you go you will find some sort of market. Markets are regular gatherings in towns or villages, once a week or once a month. The market sellers set up their stalls at each place and the local people come to buy. There may be a market every day in large towns.

Food shops often supply only one kind of food; a butcher sells meat, a baker sells bread. What others can you think of? In a small place, however, there may be only one shop, selling all kinds of food.

PREPARING FOOD

How we cook

We cook many of our foods before we eat them. Cooked food can be more easily digested, which means the body can break it down and use it more easily. Cooking also destroys bacteria in the food which could make us ill. We also cook because it allows us to change or mingle the flavour and textures of foods. And we feel warmer after a hot meal, which is important in cold weather.

Food is cooked by four methods. It can be roasted or grilled by a flame. Sometimes it is baked inside a hot, enclosed space called an oven. It can be fried, that is cooked in oil or fat. It can also be boiled or stewed in a liquid, or steamed.

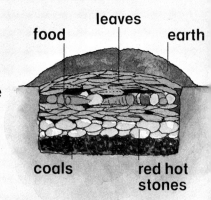

food leaves earth

coals red hot stones

Cooking in an earth oven is a very ancient practice which is still used all over the world. The food is cooked on stones on top of hot coals in a tightly-covered hole in the earth.

baking in an electric oven

stewing on an open fire

Here are some cooking and storage pots used around the world. People use whatever materials they can get — pottery, metals, plaited plant fibres, and even large leaves. What materials are used for cooking and storing food in your home?

In the beginning people probably used hot stones for cooking. They roasted food on the stones or dropped both the stones and food into a container made from the skin of an animal. When they learned to make pots from clay hardened by fire, food could be fried or boiled.

Nowadays people use all shapes and sizes of containers and all kinds of fuels and stoves. It all depends on where you live.

Some people use electricity or gas to cook their food. Others use wood, coal, charcoal or paraffin. What does your family use?

frying over a charcoal stove

spit-roasting over a wood fire

Preserving and processing food

Once people drank milk only when animals produced it in spring and summer. Then they learned to preserve it by turning it into cheese. Like milk, many foods go bad if kept for longer than a day. People used to eat them only if they were produced close to home.

For every slice of bread eaten in Britain, 30 grams of grain have been transported, cleaned, dried, and ground into flour.

Nowadays we have many ways of preserving food and carrying it by road, sea and air. We can enjoy food from far-off places. For example bananas were not available in Britain until there were specially refrigerated ships to carry them without going bad on the journey.

Many foods are processed in large factories. Here is the process in a modern bread factory.

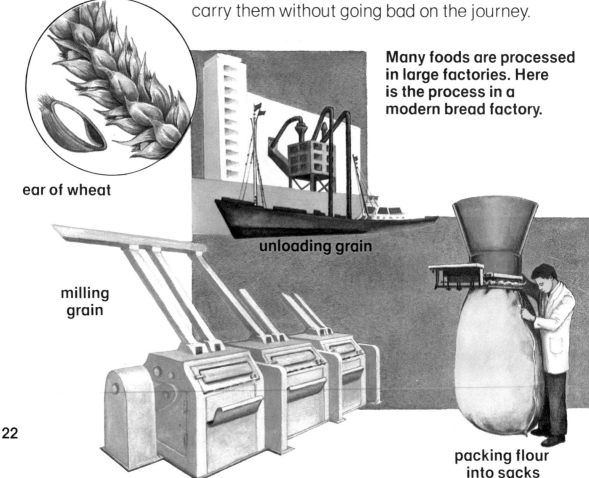

ear of wheat

unloading grain

milling grain

packing flour into sacks

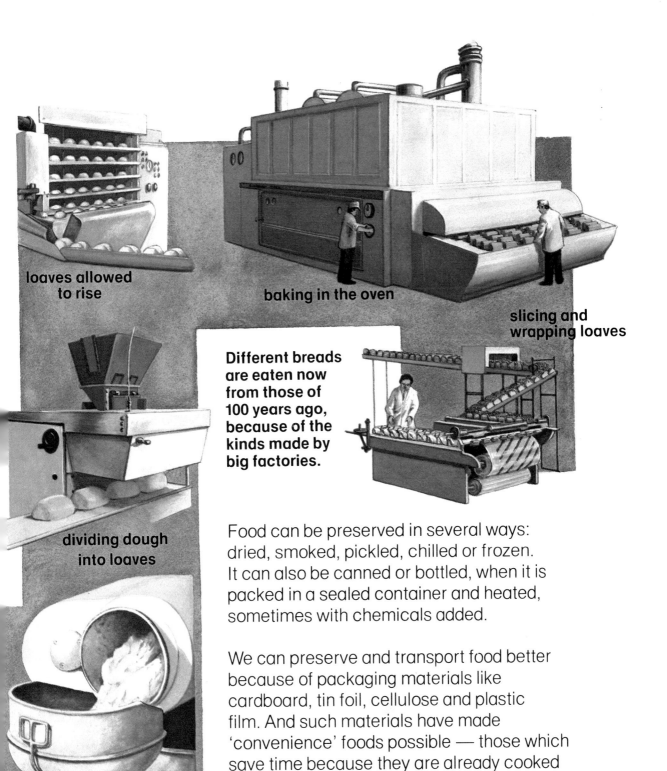

loaves allowed
to rise

baking in the oven

slicing and
wrapping loaves

**Different breads
are eaten now
from those of
100 years ago,
because of the
kinds made by
big factories.**

dividing dough
into loaves

Food can be preserved in several ways:
dried, smoked, pickled, chilled or frozen.
It can also be canned or bottled, when it is
packed in a sealed container and heated,
sometimes with chemicals added.

We can preserve and transport food better
because of packaging materials like
cardboard, tin foil, cellulose and plastic
film. And such materials have made
'convenience' foods possible — those which
save time because they are already cooked
when you buy them and only need reheating.

23

mixing flour, water
and yeast

Meals around the world

Think of a menu for a typical day's meals in your home. How many meals will you have? How many courses at each? What foods? How are they prepared and cooked?

Meals eaten in different countries may be very different. Here are some examples.

Each of the menus below is decorated with foods which are often eaten. Which do you recognise? The star marks which dish is shown.

Noodle soup.
*Tortillas filled with pork, beans and chillies. Tomato, garlic, onion and herb sauce. Salad. Mangoes and papayas.

Mexico: the local chilli pepper is used to make hot, spicy food. Meals often have many courses. Ancient Mexicans were the first to have tomatoes and chocolate. Their staple food is maize tortilla (pancake).

*Chicken curried with ginger, poppy seeds, turmeric, cardamoms, cloves, coriander. Spinach and green bean curry. Lentils. *Rice *or* chapati. Chutneys, yoghurt.

India: food is richly spiced. Many dishes are eaten at the same time. In the south, most people are vegetarians. Staple foods are flat wheat bread (chapati) and rice.

The meals people have will depend on what foods they can get, and on how they can be cooked and stored. Their customs and religion, and what foods they think are good for them, are also important. Hot or cold weather will make them want different meals. People also make their food more enjoyable by adding spices, or by decorating and arranging their meals. How do you arrange and decorate your meals?

Norway: a lot of fish is eaten either fresh or preserved by salting, pickling, smoking or freezing. Meals often include both hot and cold dishes — fish, meat, cheeses, vegetables and breads. Staple food is wheat bread.

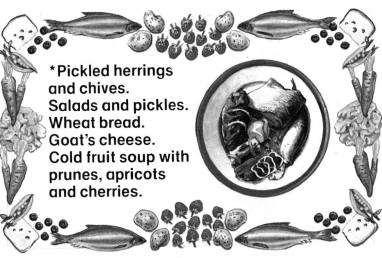

*Pickled herrings and chives. Salads and pickles. Wheat bread. Goat's cheese. Cold fruit soup with prunes, apricots and cherries.

*Bean, chicken, and pepper stew with cassava dumpling and ginger. Mangoes, pawpaws. Coconut and banana pudding.

Nigeria: home grown beans and fruit are mainly eaten, as meat is expensive. People keep chickens to provide cheaper meat. Groundnuts are grown and used in stews and cakes. Staple foods are yams and cassava.

WHERE ARE WE GOING?

Hunger in the world

Many people never eat meals like those on the previous pages. Millions of people go to sleep hungry every night of their lives. Enough food is actually produced in the world to feed everyone, but some people have too little, others have too much. Even in countries where most people get enough food, there are some who do not. These are often old people who have little money, or children who are not eating the right kinds of foods while they are growing.

There are many reasons why people do not get enough food. They may find it difficult to grow crops or keep animals successfully because of poor soil or lack of water.

It is a struggle to get enough food for the family when farming on land like this with poor soil and little water. Solving these problems may cost money which the family does not have.

One in nine people in the world suffers from starvation. They are coloured here in yellow. One in three people does not have enough of the right things to eat. They are coloured here in red.

Sometimes floods or disease can destroy crops, or there may be droughts. This is when no rain falls for many months, even for years, and no crops can grow.

Many people have no land on which to grow their own food and have to depend on others for work and wages. Some people do not have enough money to buy the food they need.

What can be done?

People who live in countries where it does not often rain can build dams to catch every drop of water and save it for times when there is drought. They can sink boreholes to draw water from deep in the earth and build channels to carry it to the land. They can treat their poor soil with fertilizers so that crops grow better.

But all this costs a lot of money and people who do not earn much from their farms are too poor to pay for it.

Crops can be improved so that they resist disease and give more food. But often the new breeds need a lot of water and expensive fertilizers.

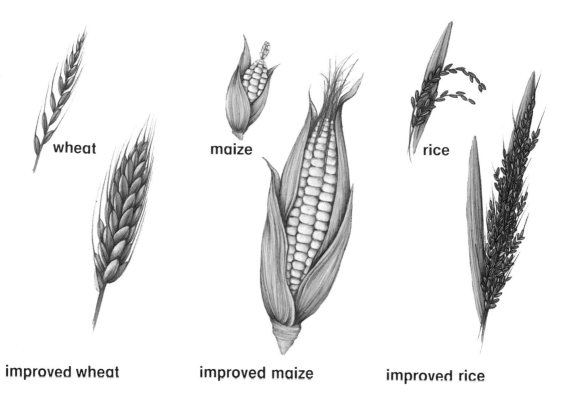

wheat

maize

rice

improved wheat

improved maize

improved rice

Millions of people do not get enough of
the nutrient called protein which helps
you grow. It is found mainly in foods
like meat, fish and eggs.

Today, new protein foods are being made
using gas, oil and plants like seaweed.
But the processes are expensive and so the
foods will not reach the people who most
need them now. What do you think should be
done so that everyone has enough food?

**Protein food being made
from bacteria which feed
on natural gas.
Top: the processing
plant turning bacteria
into food. Below: the
bacteria in their
original form.**

GLOSSARY, BOOKS TO READ

A glossary is a word list. This one explains unusual words that are used in this book.

Bacteria Very tiny living organisms which are found in almost everything. Some bacteria cause disease.

Carbohydrate One of the nutrients found in some foods, such as bread. It gives us energy.

Digest The way your body breaks food down into tiny pieces so that the food can be used by the body.

Drought A period when no rain falls for months. Water supplies get used up, no crops can grow, and animals are short of drinking water.

Factory ships Very large fishing ships which carry machines so that the fish can be cleaned, prepared and frozen on board without the ship having to return to port.

Fast A time when people do not eat at all, or do not eat certain kinds of foods, because their religion forbids it.

Fertilizers Substances which are added to soil to make plants grow better.

Nutrients Substances in food which the body takes and uses so that it can work properly.

Preserving food Treating food in some way to stop it from going bad.

Processing food A series of changes made to food to preserve it and to make it easier and faster to prepare for eating.

Protein One of the nutrients which your body needs to help you grow and stay healthy. Protein is found mainly in meat, fish, and eggs.

Staple food A main food which is eaten with most meals. For example, bread and rice are staple foods.

Vegetarian Someone who does not eat meat, only foods from plants. Some vegetarians also do not eat any other animal foods, like eggs or milk products.

Vitamins Nutrients your body needs in tiny amounts to stay healthy. Vitamins are found in many different foods.

Yeast A tiny living plant which is added to bread dough to make it rise. This means that the yeast makes bubbles of gas in the dough, so that the baked bread is light and full of holes.

BOOKS TO READ

WHAT THE WORLD EATS, Breakfast, Midday Meal, Evening Meal by Tom and Jenny Watson, Wayland 1982.
These three books describe meals eaten by people in different countries, as well as telling you a little about the kind of land and climate each country has. There are recipes for some of the dishes described.

Bread by J. P. Rutland, Franklin Watts 1982. This tells you some of the history of bread and how different breads are made. There is a recipe for making your own bread.

Food for Keeps by Heinz Kurth, Penguin 1979 (now out of print but available in many children's libraries). This book describes the different ways food is preserved and shows you ways of doing this yourself.

OLD MONEY

Barter and tokens

Can you imagine a world without money? For thousands of years people did not use money at all. They hunted animals for food, or gathered berries and nuts, and built their own dwellings. There was no need for buying and selling. In some parts of the world people still live in this way today.

These lowland farmers are exchanging their sheep for stone axe heads produced in the hills.

About 10,000 years ago, people began to settle down in one place to grow crops and keep domestic animals. Then they no longer needed to hunt for food. Instead they stayed at home, raised sheep and cattle, and baked bread.

Later, towns and cities grew up, and people settled down to different trades. Some people learned how to work metals, and became skilled toolmakers. A farmer who needed a new metal sickle to cut his barley would give the toolmaker flour in return. To avoid arguments each time, a whole system of swapping came to be agreed. In ancient Greece, a suit of bronze armour could be bought for nine oxen.

British sailors met Maori warriors during Captain Cook's 1769 expedition. Food such as lobster was bartered for European goods.

Exchanges like these are called barter. Bartering for small items was often difficult. Half a bull was of little value to anyone! Instead, people began to trade rings or other small objects such as shells, beads or animal teeth. But it was difficult for the people using them to agree on their value.

Rings, necklaces and bracelets of valuable metal were worn and kept to show their owners' wealth. Sometimes they were given as presents, or exchanged. This torc was made by Celtic craftsmen about 2000 years ago.

2400 years ago Philip II of Macedon had gold coins called staters made. These coins were copied by the Celts of what is now France.

The first coins

Traders were soon travelling far and wide. They still often bartered for goods, but usually found it easier to pay with metal tokens, which they preferred for many reasons. The metal was equally valuable wherever trade was carried out, for it was used to make tools and weapons, and pieces of metal were easy to weigh, divide or melt together. They did not wear out easily, and could be carried around or stored. In times of war they could be buried, and many of these ancient hoards have been unearthed in modern times by farmers and archaeologists.

The usual metals for tokens were gold, silver, iron, and copper. The ancient Egyptians made metal into rings, and the ancient Chinese made it into discs. Soon coins as we know them were being stamped, with pictures of oxen or wheat to show their value. Coins were also stamped with the heads of rulers, so that everyone could see how important they were. The earliest stamped coin still in existence was made over 2500 years ago for Gyges, King of Lydia.

It was much easier for a ruler to collect taxes or pay wages with coins, and so obtaining metal coins helped people to become powerful. Soon people began to think of wealth in terms of the coins themselves rather than the goods or possessions that could be bought with the money. Gold was valued above all else.

The Romans made coins from about 2300 years ago onwards, and used them for shopping and paying wages and taxes throughout their large empire.

The design of early coins was hammered on by hand, while the metal was hot. Later, presses were made to imprint cold metal. This one was in use in 1783.

The first bank notes

Coins were easy to use for everyday purposes, but they still had some disadvantages. Large numbers of coins were heavy and bulky. If rulers went to the wars, they had to carry chests and strongboxes full of money with them, in order to pay their soldiers. If they were attacked they risked losing it all.

It was far easier to leave the money behind for someone else to keep safe, and this is why the first banks grew up. In the 14th century families such as the Medicis of Florence in Italy became very wealthy by banking money, and by then lending it out to others, in return for a payment called interest.

A French painting of 600 years ago shows paper money being handed out by Chinese officials at the court of Kublai Khan.

Bankers used to give out receipts or IOUs to customers, promising to pay back the bearer of the note in coins of gold or silver. Sometimes people exchanged these paper notes without bothering to cash them in, using them instead of coins. These were the first bank notes.

The Chinese used banks and issued paper money as early as the 10th century, but it was to be over 600 years before proper bank notes were used in Europe. This only happened after banks were supported by cities and governments, so that the value of the notes they printed was guaranteed. People no longer felt they had to cash them in for gold or silver. People were suspicious of these scraps of paper at first, but soon they became as common as coins.

The Chinese note (bottom right) was in use during the Ming period (1386-1644). The Swedish note (top right) dates from 1692. The French one (bottom left) was issued in 1720, and the Bank of England note (top left) is dated 1760.

MONEY TODAY

Cash

Have a good look at your pocket money. It will be made up of coins or notes issued by the national bank of the country where you live. Most countries now use the decimal system for their money, which means that the values are based on multiples of ten. There will be coins and notes valued at 1, 5, 10, 20, 50, 100, 1000 and so on.

In some countries, such as Britain and Australia, a different system of money was once used. It was based on multiples of twelve. This was difficult to use, so the decimal system was introduced also in these countries.

The coins and notes which make up your pocket money are cash. The money is ready for spending at any time. You can save it up and put it in a bank if you want to.

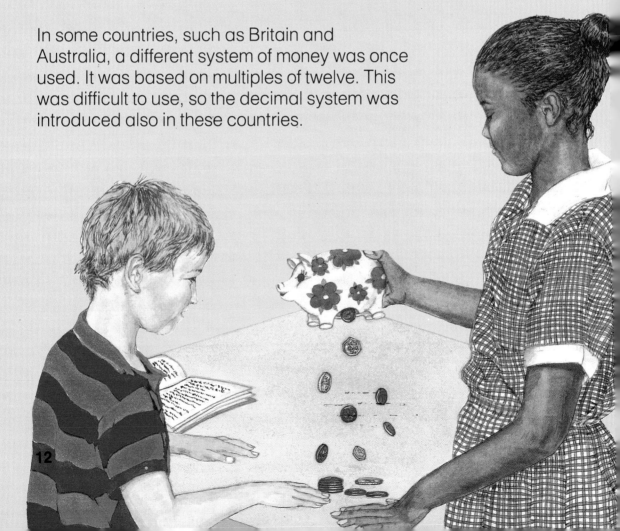

12

The kind of money used in each individual country is known as a currency. Each currency is based upon a main unit which is then divided into smaller ones. In France, for example, the franc is the main currency unit, and is divided into 100 centimes. Some units of money have special symbols, such as £ (pound or lira), and $ (dollar).

If you travel abroad, you need to have the currency of the country you visit, and so you have to change your money. Every day the banks decide upon a rate of exchange between the different currencies. One pound, for example, might be worth 1.4 US dollars, 3.6 German Deutschmark, or 198 Greek drachmas. The currency of a rich country, such as the United States of America, will be exchanged for more money than the currency of a poor country.

Japan uses a currency based on the yen. It is issued in units of 5, 10, 100, and 1000, and so is what we call a decimal currency. Coins are used for small amounts, like 5 and 10 yen, while bank notes are used for the larger amounts.

Money from metal

Coins are made in a factory called a mint, and the people in the mint have to be very careful and accurate. The modern method is fairly simple. Mint workers polish blank discs of metal until they are smooth and shiny, and then they stamp the discs in a press between two metal dies, so that the design appears clearly on both sides.

Gold and silver are today only used for special issues of coinage. Most coins are made of cheaper metals, such as copper mixed with nickel or with tin and zinc. The mixtures of metal or alloys in the coin are normally worth far less than the coin itself.

At the US mint in Philadelphia great rolls of metal await processing. They will be used to make coins.

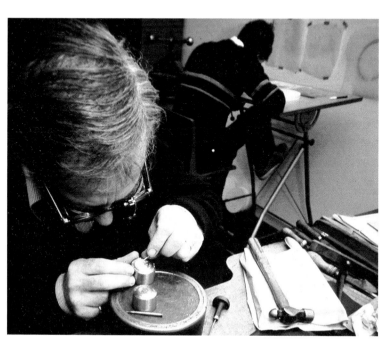

Coin dies must be engraved very precisely. They are used to stamp the pattern on coins.

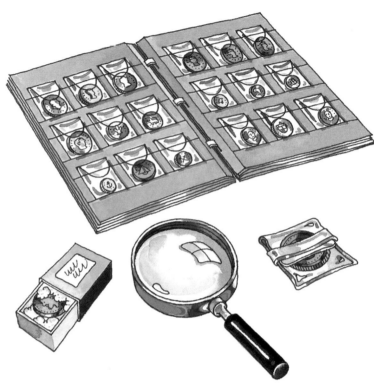

The mint must make sure that coins are not easy to copy. The original designs are modelled in clay. Moulds are taken of these and transferred to the metal dies. An engraver finishes these off in microscopic detail. Sometimes mottos or lines, called milling, are added around the rim, and these can show if the coin has been tampered with. In the past, when coins were made of valuable metal, cheats used to clip pieces from the edges.

The people who run the mint must make sure that the people who work there are honest and do not steal the coins, which are guarded carefully all the way to the bank.

Have you ever thought of becoming a numismatist? That is the name given to someone who collects coins. All you need is a magnifying glass to examine details of the coins, and an album or matchboxes to keep them in. You might try collecting old coins, or foreign coins from holidays abroad.

Paper money

Everyone would like to be able to print money for themselves. They could become rich overnight! But if money becomes too plentiful, it is not so valuable, and so the national bank of each country strictly controls the making of bank notes. Because notes are little more than printed paper, they are sometimes easy to forge, particularly using modern methods of photography and printing. To prevent forgery, the bank has to take extra care when designing bank notes. For a start, they use a special paper. This sometimes includes a pattern, called a watermark, pressed into the paper when it is made. Sometimes a metal strip is put into the paper as well.

This Iraqi bank note is worth 10 dinars. Its complicated design makes it very hard to forge.

The design printed on the notes is made up of complicated swirls and patterns, and finely engraved portraits of rulers, presidents or national heroes and heroines. These are almost impossible to copy accurately. They are printed in special coloured inks which make it very difficult to photograph the design. A serial number printed on the note helps the bank to keep track of it and check if it is genuine.

The new notes are taken to the banks under strict guard, and are soon in general use. As they become worn and tattered, the old notes are held back by the banks and replaced with crisp new ones. The old ones are then sent off to be burnt. Notes are normally of a higher value than coins, so they must be printed in secret and kept safe at all times.

Finely engraved metal plates fit around a drum for printing off sheets of bank notes. The sheets are then inspected to make sure there are no mistakes, and cut into individual bank notes.

Plastic money

Most grown-ups carry bank notes in a wallet or purse. Nowadays they often have to carry small plastic cards as well because plastic cards are now used more and more when money is exchanged, and for a number of different reasons. These cards are normally about 85 millimetres long and 55 wide, and include an embossed serial number along the bottom.

Credit cards are often used nowadays instead of cash. The shop assistant places the plastic card in a machine which prints the card number and other details on to a form. This form is sent to the credit card company as a record of the sale.

Some are known as cheque cards. A cheque is an order written on a paper form telling a bank to pay a sum of money to someone. If one of its cheque cards is presented with the cheque, the bank guarantees to make the payment.

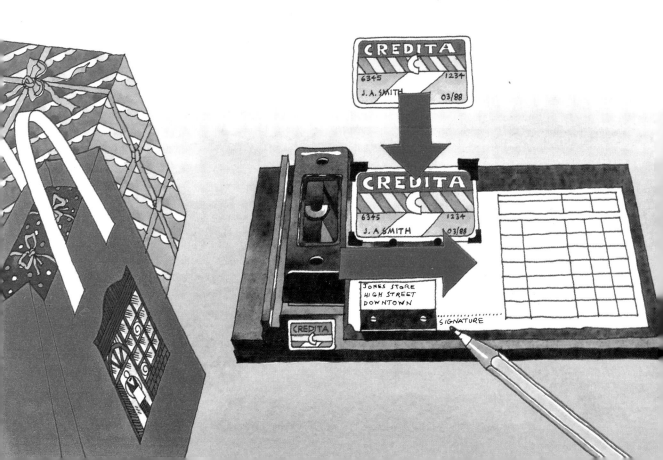

Debit cards use computers. Terminals in shops are linked electronically to the banks. Customers tap in their card number, and the money for the sale is transferred from their bank account to the shop's.

Signs displayed in a shop window show which credit cards will be accepted in payment for goods.

Cash cards are issued by the bank where you keep your money. They allow you to take out cash even when the bank is closed. All you have to do is to feed the plastic card into a machine outside the bank, a cash dispenser. Electronic equipment makes sure that the card is in order, and then delivers the bank notes.

People use credit cards to pay for goods and services because they save them the bother of carrying cash or writing out a cheque. It also means that they don't have to pay for an item immediately. Details of each credit card sale are recorded and sent to the credit card firm, and they send the bill to the card-holder.

MONEY AT WORK

Across the counter

Where do you go shopping? Perhaps you go to the shop on the corner, or to a big department store in a city. When you, or someone in your family, buys food, do you visit a supermarket, or prefer the hustle and bustle of a street market?

All these places exist so that money can be exchanged for goods. Buying and selling and earning wages all form a very important part of our lives. Have you ever stopped to think why certain goods cost more than others?

This market is in West Africa. Market traders are often prepared to offer special bargains. If a customer is able to buy a very large amount of one item, it may be worth the trader's while to charge less per item. Although she makes less profit per item, she makes more overall because more items are sold.

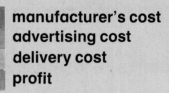

share of costs

manufacturer's cost
advertising cost
delivery cost
profit

Buying a computer game. The cost includes manufacture, advertising, delivery to the shop and profit. This picture shows how the cost breaks down.

There are many ways in which money changes hands. Let's take one example. A farmer wishes to sell eggs. The price he charges depends on how much money he has had to spend to produce the eggs. He may have needed to build henhouses, buy chicken feed, and pay wages. To all these basic costs he adds an extra sum of money called profit.

Much the same thing happens when an item is sold in a big store, only it is a little more complicated. When you buy a toy, for example, what are you paying for? First of all there is the cost of the materials used to make it, the workers' wages, the factory rent, the cost of advertising the product and the profit taken by the maker. Then there are transport, storage and delivery costs, and the profit made by the shopkeeper. Finally, part of the cost is made up of tax, a sum of money paid to the government.

Banking

Some banks are owned by the country you live in. They issue coins and notes and look after the country's money. Other banks are owned by big companies. Each bank's head office is normally in the capital city, but they have smaller branches in each town.

These banks are there to look after your savings. The money you put into a bank is called a deposit, and the money you take out is a withdrawal. The record of your deposits and withdrawals is your account and every so often the bank will send you a statement, which reminds you how much money is in your account.

You can withdraw money by filling out a cheque form. If you want the withdrawal to be paid to someone else, you write their name on the cheque.

A bank statement shows how much money is in your account. It lists each deposit and withdrawal, and any fees charged by the bank. The amount of money left in your account at any one time is called the balance.

bank statement

BiS	SPECIMEN ONLY Issued by Banking Information Service			IN ACCOUNT WITH	
TITLE OF ACCOUNT			BANK		
			BRANCH		
ACCOUNT NUMBER				STATEMENT NUMBER	
DATE	PARTICULARS	PAYMENTS	RECEIPTS	BALANCE	
	Balance Forward				

19 ____   56-81-34

cheque form

SPECIMEN

SPECIMEN

19 ____

National Westminster Bank PLC
St. Clair Branch
16 The Square, St. Clair, Norfolk

or order

£

Pay ____

PLC   LONDON, N99 4XX

SPECIMEN
19 ____
29-99-93

or order

£

£ ____
326071

⑈328071⑈ 58⑈ 8I39⑈: 00925817⑈

£ ____
239535

⑈239535⑈ 20⑈ 9993⑈: I0329985⑈

Deposits and withdrawals are made in the main hall. Some banks have an outside cash dispenser as well. Behind the counter, clerks count and weigh money, sort cheques and operate computer terminals. Money and valuables are locked up in a vault.

Banks carry out many services. They will look after valuable possessions for you, change foreign money and give you business advice. Most banks charge money for looking after your savings as well as for their other services.

In the past, bank clerks had to write down all deposits and withdrawals in a big book. Nowadays computers are used to keep a record instead.

The world of money

Throughout history people have organized the way they work, earn and spend money in different ways. Stone Age hunters and farmers did not use money at all. Later, many people worked for goods or services provided, rather than for money.

A system, or economy, which was based on private ownership and profit, grew up in most parts of the world and became known as capitalism. Many people however became unhappy with this system. They felt it would be fairer if factories and land were publicly owned. This system became known as socialism, or in some countries as communism.

In capitalist countries it is often possible for the public to buy and sell shares of a firm. If that firm does well, its value goes up, and the shareholder makes some money. People who deal in shares work in a stock exchange. This one is in Paris, France.

Today most countries have economies which are a mixture of capitalism and socialism. In countries such as China, factories and land are publicly owned, but a small amount of private business is permitted. In countries such as Britain or France, land and most businesses are privately owned, but some are owned by the state.

Different economies face different problems. Sometimes, for instance, the prices of goods in the shops start to rise very fast. This is called inflation. Prices will come down if fewer people are employed. But people who are out of work cannot afford to buy many new goods, and so less money changes hands. This means prices rise again, or more people are put out of work.

A display at a May Day parade in the Soviet Union. May Day is when socialists celebrate the workers' struggle against capitalism.

Inflation creates many problems, because you have to pay more and more money for the same thing. In 1922 this German shopkeeper had to keep a whole chest full of bank notes beside the till.

25

RICH AND POOR

The root of all evil?

An old legend tells of a king called Midas. Everything he touched turned to gold. He was the happiest man alive – until his food turned to gold as well! The moral of this tale is that money does not necessarily bring happiness.

Misers save up huge sums of money. But because they never spend it or give it away, they are unhappy. Other people can't stop gambling. However much money they lose, they still dream of winning a fortune. Other people can be so desperate for money that they rob and cheat and kill.

In the 16th century soldiers from Europe went to South America. They had heard rumours of Eldorado, a land where everything was made of gold. In their search for gold they killed the Amerindian people who lived there, and then often murdered each other too.

In the Bible it says that 'the love of money is the root of all evil'. Christian monks and nuns try to live good lives and promise to give up all personal wealth and possessions. Hindu holy men, called saddhus, live on charity alone. Do you think you would ever want to try living without money?

Buddhist monks and nuns follow the example of their great teacher, Gautama Buddha, who gave up his riches for a begging bowl. These Buddhist monks' orange robes and begging bowls show that they have chosen a life of poverty.

This Dutch picture was painted in the 17th century. It is called 'The Covetous Miser', and shows a miser with his bags of money.

Poverty and the future

Some people choose to be poor because of their religious beliefs, but many more have no choice. They cannot make enough money to pay for food or housing.

Some parts of the world are prosperous. There are factories where people can earn money, and farms producing more than enough food for all. Even in these countries there are a number of people who are poor.

In other parts of the world whole countries are poor and people are starving to death. Sometimes this is because the climate makes it hard to grow crops, or because there are droughts and floods. Some countries were once occupied by more powerful nations. They became colonies and the riches that they did produce were sometimes taken by the rulers and not given to the people who lived there. Many colonies have now become free, but they still have many problems.

Most of these poor countries are in Asia, Africa and South America. Many of the people who live there have tried to improve farming and build new roads and houses and factories. Some people from the rich countries have tried to help by giving them money or by working with them. Do you think that people in rich countries should help more?

Many African and Asian countries are very poor. When disasters such as famines happen, people may starve to death if their governments cannot help them quickly.

In 1985 young people in the richer countries of the world held a concert called Live Aid. They made a lot of money to help famine victims in Africa.

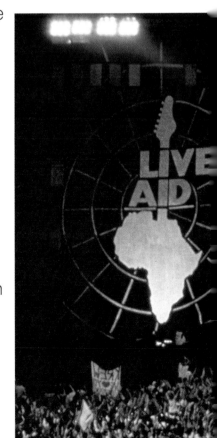

FEED THE WORLD
JULY 13th 1985 at WEMBLEY STADIUM

LIVE
AID

GLOSSARY, BOOKS TO READ

A glossary is a word list. This one explains unusual words that are used in this book.

Alloy A mixture of different metals. Coins made of alloys are cheaper to manufacture, and they are tougher.

Balance The amount of money you have left in your bank account at any one time.

Barter A form of trade in which goods are exchanged instead of being paid for with money.

Cheque A form used for withdrawing a sum of money from a bank, and for paying it to someone else.

Currency The kind of money in official use in a particular country.

Decimal Based upon ten.

Deposit A sum of money placed in a bank for safe-keeping. Deposit can also mean an advance payment.

Die An engraved metal disc used to press the design on to a coin during manufacture.

Economy Any system of organizing money, wages, manufacture, buying and selling.

Forgery Making false copies of coins or banknotes in order to cheat people.

Guarantee A way of making sure, or a promise, that something happens, such as the repayment of a loan.

Milling The small lines cut into the rim of a coin.

Mint An official factory for making coins.

Numismatist Someone who collects coins and medals.

Profit In a business deal, the amount of money left over from the sale of goods after the costs of wages, manufacture and so on have been taken away.

Tax A sum of money which must be paid to the government. It can be taken from your wages, or from property, or added on to the sale of goods.

Token An object used to represent something else. In some countries beads were once exchanged for goods. They were used as tokens.

Watermark A design pressed into the paper when it is made. It can be seen when the paper is held up to the light. Many banknotes include a watermark.

Withdrawal A sum of money taken out from a bank account.

BOOKS TO READ
Beads, Barter and Bullion by Brenda Lewis, Wayland, 1979.
Banks by Peter Lane, Batsford, 1976. Describes the history of banks in Britain
International Banking by Robert McKee, Wayland, 1981.
Money, by Richard Redden, Macdonald, 1976.
Stocks and Shares by Alan James, Batsford, 1977.
Coins and Tokens by Philip Leighton, A & C Black, 1972.
Observer's Book of British Coins by Howard Linecar, Warne, 1980.

CONTENTS

OLD MONEY 6-11

Barter and tokens 6-7

The first coins 8-9

The first bank notes 10-11

MONEY TODAY 12-19

Cash 12-13

Money from metal 14-15

Paper money 16-17

Plastic money 18-19

MONEY AT WORK 20-25

Across the counter 20-21

Banking 22-23

The world of money 24-25

RICH AND POOR 26-29

The root of all evil? 26-27

Poverty and the future 28-29

GLOSSARY, BOOKS TO READ 30

INDEX 31

How to use this book

First look at the contents page opposite. Read the chapter list to see if it includes the subject you want. The list tells you what each page is about. You can then find the page with the information you need.

If you want to know about one particular thing, look it up in the index on page 31. For example, if you want to know about credit cards, the index tells you that there is something about them on page 19. The index also lists the pictures in the book.

When you read this book, you will find some unusual words. The glossary on page 30 explains what they mean.

Series Editor Margaret Conroy

Book Editor Peter Harrison

Factual Advisor Nick Merriman

Reading Consultant Amy Gibbs

Series Design
Robert Mathias/Anne Isseyegh

Book Design Jane Robison

Production Susan Mead

Picture Research Suzanne Williams

Teacher Panel
Christine Archer, Bernadette Hill,
I.G. Richards

Illustrations
Catherine Bradbury 12-13, 20-21
Lorraine Calaora 6-7, 8-9
Jerry Collins Front cover
J. Lobban 15, 18-19, 23

Photographs
Barnes & Webster: cover
BBC Hulton Picture Library: 25B
BPCC/Aldus Archive: 6-7T, 10
British Museum: 10-11CB, 11T, 11B
Bruce Coleman/Mark Boulton: 20
Michael Holford: 9
Image Bank/Brett Froomer: 24B
National Gallery, London: 27T
Hugh Oliff: 13, 16
Rex Features: 17, 19, 24-25, 27B, 29T+B
The Royal Mint: 14
Sheridan Photo. Library: 7
Courtesy Sotheby's: 10-11CT
Spectrum: 14-15
Courtesy TSB Group: cover

MONEY

Philip Steele

Macdonald Educational

Babies 'feel' things with their mouths because lips contain lots of receptors.

receptors in your lips and fingertips than anywhere else.

You can test the touch receptors very easily. Make three touch probes with corks like the ones in the diagram. Ask a friend to close his eyes and lightly press each probe in turn on his wrist. Can he tell if you are using the probe with one, two or three pins? Take it in turns to test other areas: the inside base of your thumb, your fingertips, upper arm, or the back of your neck.

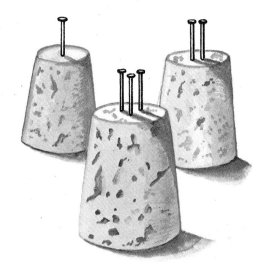

Boiling water damages your skin, and that is why it hurts. Here you can see how dangerous it is to leave pan handles within a child's reach.

Is feeling always believing?

Fill two basins, one with warm water, the other with ice-cold. Place one hand in each bowl for a few minutes. Then put the hand from the cold basin into the warm water. Does the temperature of the warm water feel the same in both hands? If not, can you work out why?

Why do you feel pain?

If you happen to be in pain right now, you might think it would be a good idea if there were no pain receptors! But is that really wise? Pain acts as a warning that something is going wrong. It protects you from further harm by making you stop what you are doing. It teaches you to take care of yourself because pain feels so unpleasant. What might happen to this little girl if the first burn didn't hurt?

Taking care of your skin

Apart from **hygiene**, there isn't much you can do. Except — and this is very important — you can take note of the information you receive. For example, if you feel too hot and you don't try to cool down, you may get **heatstroke**, which is very dangerous indeed.

Chapter 4

Smell and Taste

If you want a really good smell of something, you sniff. This pulls air up to the top of your nose. Look at the diagram and see the patch of tissue full of nerve endings. These are your smell receptors. They send information about different smells along the **olfactory nerve** to the brain. Scientists aren't sure yet how this works, but all smells are first dissolved in the watery **mucus** at the top of the nose.

There are certain smells most people like: delicious food, mown grass and clean rain. There are other smells most people find revolting, such as rotten eggs. But smells are like taste, they mean different things to different people. Some dislike the smell of tar, but others like it. Name two of your favourite smells, and two you dislike.

How smell can protect you

Smell helps you to recognize danger: fire, escaping gas, or rotting food. But you only notice a new odour for a short while — it's as if your smell receptors get used to it. This is why you can sit in a kitchen and not smell the cakes start to burn, while someone who comes in from outside will smell burning immediately.

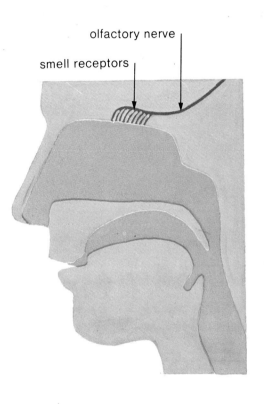

olfactory nerve

smell receptors

This man makes perfumes. His sense of smell is so sensitive he is called a 'nose'.

Some people have a much better sense of smell than others. When you have a cold you may lose your sense of smell for a while.

Your sense of taste

This seems the least important of your senses. Taste doesn't always protect you as some foods don't taste bad when they 'go off'. But taste receptors do give you a lot of pleasure — imagine not being able to taste your favourite food.

Your tongue is the organ of taste. It is covered in thousands of tiny taste buds and there are also some buds on the roof of your mouth and the back of your throat. Look in the mirror with a strong magnifying lens and you can see your taste buds.

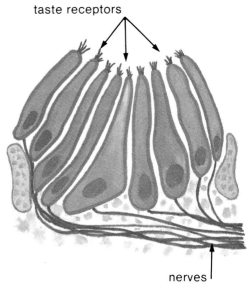

A taste bud.

Testing for taste

There are four main tastes: sweet, salt, sour and bitter. Look at the diagram and find where the taste areas are on your tongue. Most tastes are a mixture of these four. Test the different areas using sugar water, salt water, lemon juice, and strong coffee. 'Clean' your tongue between each test by eating a small piece of dry bread.

Smell and taste together

On its own, your sense of taste is very weak. It's your sense of smell which adds to the taste of food. Try this out by holding your nose before and whilst you eat.

If you lose your sense of smell when you have a cold, you might think you have lost your sense of taste, too, but you haven't. This shows how weak your sense of taste really is.

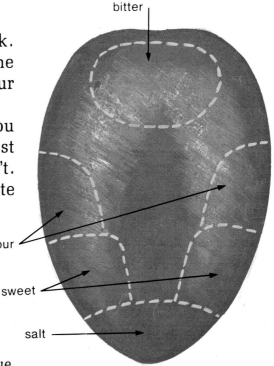

The main taste areas on your tongue.

Chapter 5

Your Ears and Hearing

Your ears collect up sounds from the outside world. There are lovely sounds, such as music, and there are also warning sounds, such as traffic approaching. But the most important sound of all is that of the human voice talking. Sight or hearing — which would you miss most?

They may not have seen the bus coming, but they will hear the driver sound his horn.

The outer parts of your ear

The **pinna**, or earlobe, picks up and directs sound into your ear. You can increase the

amount of sound collected by cupping your hand behind your ear.

The canal directs sound to your **ear-drum**. In the canal are tiny hairs and a waxy fluid which traps dirt and keeps the canal clean.

The inner parts of your ear

Your ear-drum is a sheet of skin and muscle tightly stretched over the end of the canal. The **middle ear** behind your ear-drum is filled with air, which comes up the **Eustachian tube** from your throat. The

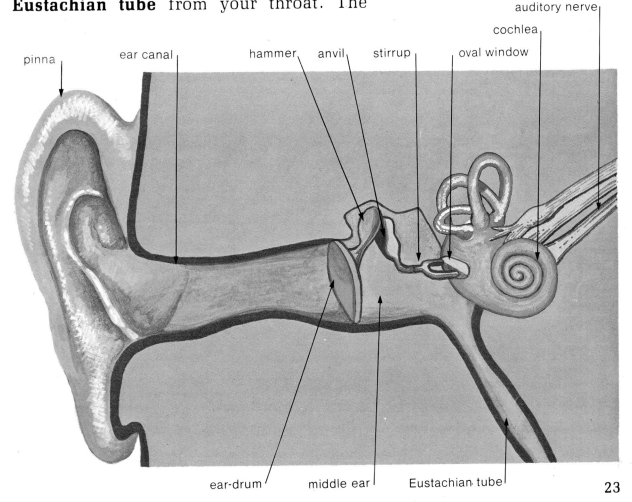

three tiny bones, the **hammer**, **anvil** and **stirrup**, make a link across the middle ear — can you see why they have these names? The **oval window** is, in fact, another sheet of skin and is part of the **cochlea**. The cochlea looks like a snail's shell and is about the size of a pea. It is filled with fluid and nerve endings.

How do you hear sounds?

Sound travels down the canal and starts the ear-drum vibrating. The three tiny bones pick up the vibrations and magnify them. The vibration passes on to the oval window, which then makes the fluid in the cochlea vibrate. The tiny nerve endings in the cochlea are your sound receptors. They pass sound information to your brain along the **auditory nerve**. Your brain interprets the information as sounds.

Why do your ears 'pop'?

On the diagram of the ear, find the Eustachian tube. Now swallow hard and you will hear a 'popping' sound in your head. Swallowing opens the tube, letting air in or out of your middle ear so that the air pressure is always the same on both sides of your ear-drum.

When you take off or land in a plane, the air pressure outside your ear-drum changes. This can feel uncomfortable and cause slight deafness. Swallow hard a few times and the feeling will wear off. You have helped the air pressure stay the same inside and outside your ear-drum.

Your ears 'pop' as you go up or come down in a plane.

Two ears are better than one

You can test this by carrying out an experiment with a friend. Your friend must be blindfolded and have one ear covered up. Now gently tap a tin can, moving further away and backwards on your friend's 'deaf' side. Note when your friend stops hearing. Is he sure where you are? If you do this again with both ears uncovered you will notice that two ears not only pick up more sound, but they also help you to judge which direction the sounds are coming from.

How we learn to speak

The most important sounds you hear are speech. At first, babies just coo and gurgle. Then they imitate the sounds made by grown-ups. All speech is learned this way, first by copying and then by practising the sounds of words. Can you guess why it is very important for parents to talk to their babies? What would happen if a baby never heard the sound of a human voice?

Playing a game blindfolded means you have to rely on your ears instead of your eyes.

These two deaf children are learning to communicate through sign language.

Deafness

Complete or 'profound' deafness is unusual. But a person who is only partly deaf finds it difficult to learn to speak. Cover your ears and imagine how shut off and lonely a deaf person might feel. Which sounds do you think you would probably miss most?

Hearing aids can magnify sounds and help some kinds of deafness. Lip-reading is useful, but the deaf person must be able to see the lips of the person speaking. Sign language is a good way to communicate. Sadly, not many hearing people learn it.

It is not unusual for old people to become a little deaf. They cannot hear high-pitched sound. Keep your voice low.

Your sense of balance

Your brain needs information about your position in space — whether you are upright, leaning forward, or lying down. The sense organs which collect up this information are inside your **inner ear**. They are called the **semicircular canals**.

Study the diagram and notice that each canal lies in a different position. If you could open one up, you would see it is filled with fluid and lined with tiny hairs. When you move your head, the fluid in all three canals moves as well. The tiny hairs are balance receptors, and they send information about the movements of the fluid to your brain.

Your eyes and your stretch receptors [see page 6] also help with your sense of balance. They send information to your brain at the same time as the canals. A person may be travel-sick because his brain is confused by differing information coming in. His eyes may tell him he is sitting still, but going over bumps will make the fluid in his inner ear move, and send the opposite information to the brain.

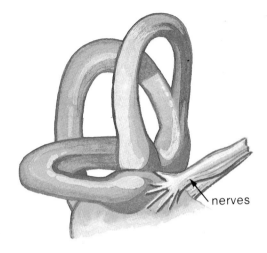

nerves

The semicircular canals.

The rides at a fairground are fun, but it is dangerous to spin round on the spot too fast. When you stop spinning, the fluid in the canals is still moving, but your brain is getting different information from your legs and eyes. This makes you feel very giddy. You may even fall over.

Why will these two chidren feel a bit giddy when the ride stops?

Taking care of your ears and hearing

The most usual kind of infection in the ear is a 'middle ear infection'. Germs can easily travel up the Eustachian tube to the ear — especially when you have a cold. Don't blow your nose too hard as this can force the cold germs up the tube. Go to the doctor if your ears start to hurt.

Sometimes ear wax hardens and blocks the ear canal, making you slightly deaf. But you should never try to get it out with your finger or cotton wool buds. A little warm cooking oil will soften the wax and help it come out naturally.

If you live in a city, you are likely to be surrounded by noise: aircraft, cars, motorbikes and building works. Wherever you are, close your eyes and listen very carefully. How many different sounds can you hear?

Very loud noise can damage your hearing — this is noise pollution. People who work with noisy machinery should wear ear protectors for safety. Too much noise going on for too long can give you a headache. It also spoils your concentration and puts you in a bad mood.

Take care of all your senses — they are the 'gateways to your brain'.

The doctor is using an instrument with a light in it to check this little girl's ear-drum.

Glossary

auditory nerve The bundle of nerves which carries information from the **semicircular canals** and the **cochlea** to the brain.

braille Special printing for the blind in which letters are made of raised dots. These are read by feeling them with the fingertips.

binocular vision The ability to see an object with both eyes at once. Creatures with eyes on the sides of their heads do not have binocular vision.

cochlea The spiral-shaped organ of hearing in your **inner ear**.

cones The light **receptors** in your **retina** which pick up colour.

conjunctiva The thin transparent covering of the inside of your eyelids and front of your eye.

conjunctivitis An infection of the **conjunctiva**; sometimes called 'pink eye'.

contagious As in contagious disease; a disease which can be spread from one person to another by touching.

ear-drum The sheet of skin which stretches across the end of your ear canal.

Eustachian tube The passage, about 4 cm (1½ inches) long, which connects your **middle ear** with the back of your throat.

focus To see something clearly — your **lens** brings together the rays of light falling into your eye so that they focus sharply on your **retina**.

hammer, anvil and stirrup The names of the three tiny bones in your **middle ear**.

heatstroke An illness caused by your body overheating.

hygiene The rules of health and cleanliness.

inner ear The part of your ear which is inside your skull. It contains the **cochlea** (for hearing) and **semicircular canals** (for balance).

iris The coloured part of your eye.

lens This is the round, flat transparent part of your eye behind your **pupil**. It will focus the light coming into your eye.

ligaments The bands of fibre which move the **lens** in your eye. You can read more about ligaments in another book in this series — **The Structure of Your Body**.

middle ear The air-filled section behind your **ear-drum**. It contains the three tiny bones called the **hammer**, **anvil** and **stirrup**.

mucus A watery fluid produced in various parts of your body, including your nose.

olfactory This means 'connected with the sense of smell', as in the olfactory nerves in your nose.

optical illusion A picture or object which misleads your brain into 'seeing' something which isn't there.

optic nerve The bundle of nerves which carries information from the **rods** and **cones** of your **retina** to your brain.

oval window The sheet of skin on the surface of the **cochlea**. It carries the vibrations from your **middle ear** into your **inner ear**.

pinna The visible part of your ear; your earlobe.

pupil The round hole in the middle of your eye which lets in the light.

receptors Nerve endings in your sense organs and muscles. They collect up information.

retina The thin layer of nerve cells at the back of your eye which are sensitive to light and colour.

refract To bend or change the direction of a beam of light.

rods The light **receptors** in your eye which pick up dim light and enable you to see in the dark.

semicircular canals The three canals in your **inner ear**. They send information to your brain to control your sense of balance.

stimulus Something which triggers off a reaction, such as a bright light making the **pupil** of your eye close up.

stretch receptors Nerve endings which collect up information about what is going on inside you.

stye A tiny boil in one of the oil glands at the edge of your eyelid.

Index

anvil bone 24
auditory nerve 24

babies 6, 11, 16, 25
balance 5, 27-8
binocular vision 12
blindness 7, 13, 16
  colour blindness 13
blind spot 10
blinking 7,8
bones 24
braille 13
brain 5, 6, 9, 10, 12,
  16, 24, 27, 28

check-ups 13, 15
cochlea 24
colds 20, 21, 29
colour blindness 13
cones 9, 10, 13
conjunctiva 7
conjunctivitis 14
contagious 14
crying 8

deafness 24, 26-7, 29

ears 5, 22-7, 29
  ear bones 24
  ear canal 23, 24
  ear-drum 23, 24-5
  ear-lobe 22
Eustachian tube 23,
  24, 29

eyes 5, 7-15
  eyeball 7, 10, 11
  eyebrows 7
  eyelashes 7, 14
  eyelids 7, 14
  eye muscles 11, 14
  eye test 13

focussing 9, 14
food 19, 20, 21

germs 14, 29
glasses 14

hammer, anvil and
  stirrup 24
hearing 5, 22-7, 29
hearing aid 26
heatstroke 18
hygiene 18

infections 14, 29
inner ear 5, 27
iris 8-9

lens 9, 14
ligaments 9
lipreading 26
lips 16, 17
long-sighted 14

middle ear 23-4, 29
mouth 16, 21
mucus 19

muscle 6, 8, 9, 23
  eye muscles 11, 14

nerve endings 5, 6, 9,
  19, 24
  cones 9, 10, 13
  rods 9, 10
nerves 5, 6
  olfactory nerve 19
  optic nerve 9, 10
noise 29
nose 5, 8, 11, 19, 21,
  29

olfactory nerve 19
optical illusions 10
optician 14
optic nerve 9, 10
organs 5, 6, 21, 27
oval window 24

pain 16, 18
'pink-eye' 14
pinna 22
protection 6, 7, 15, 18,
  19, 20, 29
pupil 8, 9

receptors 5, 6, 9, 16,
  17, 18, 19, 20, 24, 27
refract 9
retina 9, 14
rods 9, 10

semicircular canals
  27-8
sense organs 5, 6, 21,
  27
short-sighted 14
sight 4, 7-15, 22
sign language 27
skin 5, 16, 23, 24
smell 5, 19-21
sounds 22-6
spectacles 14
speech 25, 26
squint 11
stimulus 5, 6
stirrup bone 24
stretch receptors 6, 27
stye 14

taste 5, 19-21
taste buds 21
tear ducts 8
tear glands 8
tears 8, 14
temperature 18
throat 21, 23
tongue 5, 21
touch 5, 13, 16-18
travel sickness 27

vitamins 15
voice 22, 25, 27

Picture Acknowledgements Sally and Richard Greenhill 4, 5, 6, 15, 22, 24, 25, 26, 28;
Picturepoint 12, 18; Rex Features 13; Science Photo Library 8; Wayland Picture Library 14, 20,
29; Zefa 17.